You know the Bible has help for every situation. But sometimes it's hard to find the time to look up the appropriate verse. This handy guide is packed full of the Scripture you need—all presented in an easy-to-use manner. Whatever your concern—whether you are feeling angry, lonely, or weak—you can find the help you need here. Quickly. When you need it—not fifteen minutes later. You'll want to carry this book with you, leave it in a handy place at home, or give it to someone you love.

BY M. J. Capley:
Bible Puzzles and Games
More Bible Puzzles and Games
Revell's Ready-Reference Guide

Revell's
Ready-Reference
Guide

M. J. Capley

SPIRE BOOKS
Fleming H. Revell Company
Old Tappan, New Jersey

Scripture quotations are from the King James Version of the Bible.

ISBN 0-8007-8445-6
Printed in the United States of America
This is an original Spire Book, published by Spire Books,
a division of Fleming H. Revell Company,
Old Tappan, New Jersey

Contents

5

Humility	Pride
Hypocrisy	Quenching
Idolatry	Quietness
Impatience	Refuge
Imperfection	Renewal
Indiscretion	Robbery
Inferiority	Satan
Inhospitality	Selfishness
Intemperance	Shame
Judging	Sickness
Justification	Sin
Killing	Slander
Knowledge	Sorrow
Laziness	Speech
Loneliness	Strife
Lust	Temptation
Lying	Tithing
Marriage	Tribulation
Meekness	Trouble
Mercy	Uncleanness
Mind	Understanding
Money	Vengeance
Need	Vigilance
Neighbors	Weakness
Noise	Widow
Obedience	Wisdom
Oppression	Worry
Persecution	Worship
Poverty	Xenophobia
Praise	Yoke
Prayer	Youth
Prejudice	Zeal

Revell's
Ready-Reference
Guide

Adultery

Exodus 20:14—Thou shalt not commit adultery.

Proverbs 6:32—But whoso committeth adultery with a woman lacketh understanding: he that doeth it destroyeth his own soul.

Romans 12:1—I beseech you therefore, brethren, by the mercies of God, that ye present your bodies a living sacrifice, holy, acceptable unto God, which is your reasonable service.

1 Corinthians 6:9—Know ye not that the unrighteous shall not inherit the kingdom of God? Be not deceived: neither fornicators, nor idolaters, nor adulterers, nor effeminate, nor abusers of themselves with mankind.

Hebrews 13:4—Marriage is honourable in all, and the bed undefiled: but whoremongers and adulterers God will judge.

James 4:4—Ye adulterers and adulteresses, know ye not that the friendship of the world is enmity with God? whosoever therefore will be a friend of the world is the enemy of God.

Affliction

2 Samuel 22:28—And the afflicted people thou wilt save: but thine eyes are upon the haughty, that thou mayest bring them down.

Psalms 18:27—For thou wilt save the afflicted people; but wilt bring down high looks.

Psalms 34:19—Many are the afflictions of the righteous: but the Lord delivereth him out of them all.

Psalms 119:50—This is my comfort in my affliction: for thy word hath quickened me.

Isaiah 49:13—Sing, O heavens; and be joyful, O earth; and break forth into singing, O mountains: for the Lord hath comforted his people, and will have mercy upon his afflicted.

Lamentations 3:31-33—For the Lord will not cast off for ever: But though he cause grief, yet will he have compassion according to the multitude of his mercies. For he doth not afflict willingly nor grieve the children of men.

James 5:13—Is any among you afflicted? let him pray. Is any merry? let him sing psalms.

Anger

Psalms 37:8—Cease from anger, and forsake wrath: fret not thyself in any wise to do evil.

Proverbs 15:1—A soft answer turneth away wrath: but grievous words stir up anger.

Proverbs 15:18—A wrathful man stirreth up strife: but he that is slow to anger appeaseth strife.

Proverbs 16:32—He that is slow to anger is better than the mighty; and he that ruleth his spirit than he that taketh a city.

Proverbs 29:22—An angry man stirreth up strife, and a furious man aboundeth in transgression.

Ecclesiastes 7:9—Be not hasty in thy spirit to be angry: for anger resteth in the bosom of fools.

Ephesians 4:26—Be ye angry, and sin not: let not the sun go down upon your wrath.

James 1:19—Wherefore, my beloved brethren, let every man be swift to hear, slow to speak, slow to wrath.

Asking

Matthew 6:8—Be not ye therefore like unto them: for your Father knoweth what things ye have need of, before ye ask him.

Matthew 7:7—Ask, and it shall be given you; seek, and ye shall find; knock, and it shall be opened unto you.

Matthew 7:11—If ye then, being evil, know how to give good gifts unto your children, how much more shall your Father which is in heaven give good things to them that ask him?

Matthew 18:19—Again I say unto you, That if two of you shall agree on earth as touching any thing that they shall ask, it shall be done for them of my Father which is in heaven.

John 14:14—If ye shall ask any thing in my name, I will do it.

John 15:7—If ye abide in me, and my words abide in you, ye shall ask what ye will, and it shall be done unto you.

John 16:24—Hitherto have ye asked nothing in my name: ask, and ye shall receive, that your joy may be full.

Ephesians 3:20—Now unto him that is able to do exceeding abundantly above all that we ask or think, according to the power that worketh in us.

James 4:3—Ye ask, and receive not, because ye ask amiss, that ye may consume it upon your lusts.

1 John 3:22—And whatsoever we ask, we receive of him, because we keep his commandments, and do those things that are pleasing in his sight.

1 John 5:14—And this is the confidence that we have in him, that, if we ask any thing according to his will, he heareth us.

B

Backsliding

Proverbs 14:14—The backslider in heart shall be filled with his own ways: and a good man shall be satisfied from himself.

Jeremiah 3:14—Turn, O backsliding children, saith the Lord; for I am married unto you: and I will take you one of a city, and two of a family, and I will bring you to Zion.

Hosea 14:4—I will heal their backsliding, I will love them freely: for mine anger is turned away from him.

Barrenness

Deuteronomy 7:14—Thou shalt be blessed above all people: there shall not be male or female barren among you, or among your cattle.

Deuteronomy 28:4—Blessed shall be the fruit of thy body, and the fruit of thy ground, and the fruit of thy cattle, the increase of thy kine, and the flocks of thy sheep.

Deuteronomy 30:9—And the Lord thy God will make thee plenteous in every work of thine hand, in the fruit of thy body, and in the fruit of thy cattle, and in the fruit of thy land, for good: for the Lord will again rejoice over thee for good, as he rejoiced over thy fathers.

Job 5:25—Thou shalt know also that thy seed shall be great, and thine offspring as the grass of the earth.

Psalms 113:9—He maketh the barren woman to keep house, and to be a joyful mother of children. Praise ye the Lord.

Blasphemy

Psalms 74:18—Remember this, that the enemy hath reproached, O Lord, and that the foolish people have blasphemed thy name.

Matthew 12:31—Wherefore I say unto you, All manner of sin and blasphemy shall be forgiven unto men:

but the blasphemy against the Holy Ghost shall not be forgiven unto men.

Mark 7:22, 23—Thefts, covetousness, wickedness, deceit, lasciviousness, an evil eye, blasphemy, pride, foolishness: All these evil things come from within, and defile the man.

Colossians 3:8—But now ye also put off all these: anger, wrath, malice, blasphemy, filthy communication out of your mouth.

1 Timothy 6:1—Let as many servants as are under the yoke count their own masters worthy of all honour, that the name of God and his doctrine be not blas- - phemed.

Boasting

Psalms 44:8—In God we boast all the day long, and praise thy name for ever.

Proverbs 27:1—Boast not thyself of to morrow; for thou knowest not what a day may bring forth.

Ephesians 2:8, 9—For by grace are ye saved through faith; and that not of yourselves: it is the gift of God: Not of works, lest any man should boast.

James 3:5—Even so the tongue is a little member, and boasteth great things. Behold, how great a matter a little fire kindleth!

Boldness

Psalms 31:24—Be of good courage, and he shall strengthen your heart, all ye that hope in the Lord.

Proverbs 28:1—The wicked flee when no man pursueth: but the righteous are bold as a lion.

Ephesians 3:11, 12—According to the eternal purpose which he purposed in Christ Jesus our Lord: In whom we have boldness and access with confidence by the faith of him.

Hebrews 4:16—Let us therefore come boldly unto the throne of grace, that we may obtain mercy, and find grace to help in time of need.

Hebrews 10:19—Having therefore, brethren, boldness to enter into the holiest by the blood of Jesus.

Bondage

Psalms 18:2—The Lord is my rock, and my fortress, and my deliverer; my God, my strength, in whom I will trust; my buckler, and the horn of my salvation, and my high tower.

Psalms 68:6—God setteth the solitary in families: he bringeth out those which are bound with chains: but the rebellious dwell in a dry land.

Psalms 146:7—Which executeth judgment for the oppressed: which giveth food to the hungry. The Lord looseth the prisoners.

Isaiah 5:13—Therefore my people are gone into captivity, because they have no knowledge: and their honourable men are famished, and their multitude dried up with thirst.

John 8:32—And ye shall know the truth, and the truth shall make you free.

John 8:36—If the Son therefore shall make you free, ye shall be free indeed.

2 Corinthians 3:17—Now the Lord is that Spirit: and where the Spirit of the Lord is, there is liberty.

Borrowing

Deuteronomy 28:12—The Lord shall open unto thee his good treasure, the heaven to give the rain unto thy land in his season, and to bless all the work of thine hand: and thou shalt lend unto many nations, and thou shalt not borrow.

Psalms 37:21—The wicked borroweth, and payeth not again: but the righteous sheweth mercy, and giveth.

Psalms 112:5—A good man sheweth favour, and lendeth: he will guide his affairs with discretion.

Proverbs 22:7—The rich ruleth over the poor, and the borrower is servant to the lender.

Matthew 5:42—Give to him that asketh thee, and from him that would borrow of thee turn not thou away.

Romans 13:8—Owe no man any thing, but to love one another: for he that loveth another hath fulfilled the law.

C

Chastening

Proverbs 3:11, 12—My son, despise not the chastening of the Lord; neither be weary of his correction: For whom the Lord loveth he correcteth; even as a father the son in whom he delighteth.

Proverbs 13:18—Poverty and shame shall be to him that refuseth instruction: but he that regardeth reproof shall be honoured.

1 Corinthians 11:32—But when we are judged, we are chastened of the Lord, that we should not be condemned with the world.

Hebrews 12:10, 11—For they verily for a few days chastened us after their own pleasure; but he for our profit, that we might be partakers of his holiness. Now no chastening for the present seemeth to be joyous, but grievous: nevertheless afterward it yieldeth the peaceable fruit of righteousness unto them which are exercised thereby.

Revelation 3:19—As many as I love, I rebuke and chasten: be zealous therefore, and repent.

Comfort

Psalms 23:4—Yea, though I walk through the valley of the shadow of death, I will fear no evil: for thou art with me; thy rod and thy staff they comfort me.

John 14:26—But the Comforter, which is the Holy Ghost, whom the Father will send in my name, he shall teach you all things, and bring all things to your remembrance, whatsoever I have said unto you.

2 Corinthians 1:3, 4—Blessed be God, even the Father of our Lord Jesus Christ, the Father of mercies, and the God of all comfort; Who comforteth us in all our tribulation, that we may be able to comfort them which are in any trouble, by the comfort wherewith we ourselves are comforted of God.

1 Thessalonians 4:17, 18—Then we which are alive and remain shall be caught up together with them in the clouds, to meet the Lord in the air: and so shall we ever be with the Lord. Wherefore comfort one another with these words.

1 Thessalonians 5:11—Wherefore comfort yourselves together, and edify one another, even as also ye do.

2 Thessalonians 2:16, 17—Now our Lord Jesus Christ himself, and God, even our Father, which hath loved us, and hath given us everlasting consolation and good hope through grace, Comfort your hearts, and stablish you in every good word and work.

Complaining

Numbers 11:1—And when the people complained, it displeased the Lord: and the Lord heard it; and his anger was kindled; and the fire of the Lord burnt among them, and consumed them that were in the uttermost parts of the camp.

Lamentations 3:39, 40—Wherefore doth a living man complain, a man for the punishment of his sins? Let us search and try our ways, and turn again to the Lord.

1 Corinthians 10:10—Neither murmur ye, as some of them also murmured, and were destroyed of the destroyer.

Jude 16—These are murmurers, complainers, walking after their own lusts; and their mouth speaketh great swelling words, having men's persons in admiration because of advantage.

Confusion

Psalms 35:4—Let them be confounded and put to shame that seek after my soul: let them be turned back and brought to confusion that devise my hurt.

Psalms 71:1—In thee, O Lord, do I put my trust: let me never be put to confusion.

1 Corinthians 14:33—For God is not the author of confusion, but of peace, as in all churches of the saints.

Covetousness

Exodus 20:17—Thou shalt not covet thy neighbour's house, thou shalt not covet thy neighbour's wife, nor his manservant, nor his maidservant, nor his ox, nor his ass, nor any thing that is thy neighbour's.

Psalms 10:3—For the wicked boasteth of his heart's desire, and blesseth the covetous, whom the Lord abhorreth.

Proverbs 28:16—The prince that wanteth understanding is also a great oppressor: but he that hateth covetousness shall prolong his days.

Luke 12:15—And he said unto them, Take heed, and beware of covetousness: for a man's life consisteth not in the abundance of the things which he possesseth.

1 Corinthians 6:10—Nor thieves, nor covetous, nor drunkards, nor revilers, nor extortioners, shall inherit the kingdom of God.

1 Corinthians 12:31—But covet earnestly the best gifts: and yet shew I unto you a more excellent way.

1 Corinthians 14:39—Wherefore, brethren, covet to prophesy, and forbid not to speak with tongues.

Ephesians 5:5—For this ye know, that no whoremonger, nor unclean person, nor covetous man, who is an idolater, hath any inheritance in the kingdom of Christ and of God.

D

Death

Deuteronomy 30:19—I call heaven and earth to record this day against you, that I have set before you life and death, blessing and cursing: therefore choose life, that both thou and thy seed may live.

Job 5:20—In famine he shall redeem thee from death: and in war from the power of the sword.

Proverbs 10:2—Treasures of wickedness profit nothing: but righteousness delivereth from death.

Proverbs 12:28—In the way of righteousness is life; and in the pathway thereof there is no death.

Proverbs 29:18—Where there is no vision, the people perish: but he that keepeth the law, happy is he.

Matthew 26:52—Then said Jesus unto him, Put up again thy sword into his place: for all they that take the sword shall perish with the sword.

John 5:24—Verily, verily, I say unto you, He that heareth my word, and believeth on him that sent me, hath everlasting life, and shall not come into condemnation; but is passed from death unto life.

Romans 6:3, 4—Know ye not, that so many of us as were baptized into Jesus Christ were baptized into his death? Therefore we are buried with him by baptism into death: that like as Christ was raised up from the dead by the glory of the Father, even so we also should walk in newness of life.

Romans 8:2—For the law of the Spirit of life in Christ Jesus hath made me free from the law of sin and death.

Romans 8:6—For to be carnally minded is death; but to be spiritually minded is life and peace.

2 Timothy 1:10—But is now made manifest by the appearing of our Saviour Jesus Christ, who hath abolished death, and hath brought life and immortality to light through the gospel.

Deception

Deuteronomy 11:16—Take heed to yourselves, that your heart be not deceived, and ye turn aside, and serve other gods, and worship them.

Proverbs 24:28—Be not a witness against thy neighbour without cause; and deceive not with thy lips.

Obadiah 3—The pride of thine heart hath deceived thee, thou that dwellest in the clefts of the rock, whose habitation is high; that saith in his heart, Who shall bring me down to the ground?

Matthew 24:23, 24—Then if any man shall say unto you, Lo, here is Christ, or there; believe it not. For there shall arise false Christs, and false prophets, and shall shew great signs and wonders; insomuch that, if it were possible, they shall deceive the very elect.

Galatians 6:7—Be not deceived; God is not mocked: for whatsoever a man soweth, that shall he also reap.

Colossians 2:8—Beware lest any man spoil you through philosophy and vain deceit, after the tradition of men, after the rudiments of the world, and not after Christ.

2 Thessalonians 2:3, 4—Let no man deceive you by any means: for that day shall not come, except there come a falling away first, and that man of sin be revealed, the son of perdition; Who opposeth and exalteth himself above all that is called God, or that is worshipped; so that he as God sitteth in the temple of God, shewing himself that he is God.

James 1:26—If any man among you seem to be religious, and bridleth not his tongue, but deceiveth his own heart, this man's religion is vain.

Defeat

Luke 10:19—Behold, I give unto you power to tread on serpents and scorpions, and over all the power of the enemy: and nothing shall by any means hurt you.

Romans 8:37—Nay, in all these things we are more than conquerors through him that loved us.

1 Corinthians 15:57—But thanks be to God, which giveth us the victory through our Lord Jesus Christ.

1 John 4:4—Ye are of God, little children, and have overcome them: because greater is he that is in you, than he that is in the world.

1 John 5:4—For whatsoever is born of God overcometh the world: and this is the victory that overcometh the world, even our faith.

Desires

Psalms 37:4—Delight thyself also in the Lord; and he shall give thee the desires of thine heart.

Psalms 112:10—The wicked shall see it, and be grieved; he shall gnash with his teeth, and melt away: the desire of the wicked shall perish.

Psalms 118:7—The Lord taketh my part with them that help me: therefore shall I see my desire upon them that hate me.

Psalms 145:16—Thou openest thine hand, and satisfiest the desire of every living thing.

Psalms 145:18, 19—The Lord is nigh unto all them that call upon him, to all that call upon him in truth. He will fulfil the desire of them that fear him: he also will hear their cry, and will save them.

Proverbs 10:24—The fear of the wicked, it shall come upon him: but the desire of the righteous shall be granted.

Proverbs 13:12—Hope deferred maketh the heart sick: but when the desire cometh, it is a tree of life.

Mark 11:24—Therefore I say unto you, What things soever ye desire, when ye pray, believe that ye receive them, and ye shall have them.

Destruction

Job 5:22—At destruction and famine thou shalt laugh: neither shalt thou be afraid of the beasts of the earth.

Psalms 103:4—Who redeemeth thy life from destruction; who crowneth thee with lovingkindness and tender mercies.

Psalms 107:20—He sent his word, and healed them, and delivered them from their destructions.

Proverbs 10:29—The way of the Lord is strength to the upright: but destruction shall be to the workers of iniquity.

Proverbs 13:13—Whoso despiseth the word shall be destroyed: but he that feareth the commandment shall be rewarded.

Proverbs 18:7—A fool's mouth is his destruction, and his lips are the snare of his soul.

Malachi 3:11—And I will rebuke the devourer for your sakes, and he shall not destroy the fruits of your ground; neither shall your vine cast her fruit before the time in the field, saith the Lord of hosts.

Devils

Mark 16:17—And these signs shall follow them that believe; In my name shall they cast out devils; they shall speak with new tongues.

Luke 10:20—Notwithstanding in this rejoice not, that the spirits are subject unto you; but rather rejoice, because your names are written in heaven.

Ephesians 6:12—For we wrestle not against flesh and blood, but against principalities, against powers, against the rulers of the darkness of this world, against spiritual wickedness in high places.

Colossians 2:10—And ye are complete in him, which is the head of all principality and power.

James 2:19—Thou believest that there is one God; thou doest well: the devils also believe, and tremble.

Discipline

Proverbs 13:24—He that spareth his rod hateth his son: but he that loveth him chasteneth him betimes.

Proverbs 15:10—Correction is grievous unto him that forsaketh the way: and he that hateth reproof shall die.

Proverbs 19:18—Chasten thy son while there is hope, and let not thy soul spare for his crying.

Proverbs 22:6—Train up a child in the way he should go: and when he is old, he will not depart from it.

Proverbs 22:15—Foolishness is bound in the heart of a child; but the rod of correction shall drive it far from him.

Proverbs 23:13, 14—Withhold not correction from the child: for if thou beatest him with the rod, he shall not die. Thou shalt beat him with the rod, and shalt deliver his soul from hell.

Proverbs 29:17—Correct thy son, and he shall give thee rest; yea, he shall give delight unto thy soul.

Disobedience

Deuteronomy 11:26, 27—Behold, I set before you this day a blessing and a curse; A blessing, if ye obey the commandments of the Lord your God, which I command you this day.

Deuteronomy 28:1—And it shall come to pass, if thou shalt hearken diligently unto the voice of the Lord thy God, to observe and to do all his commandments which I command thee this day, that the Lord thy God will set thee on high above all nations of the earth.

Proverbs 3:1, 2—My son, forget not my law; but let thine heart keep my commandments: For length of days, and long life, and peace, shall they add to thee.

Ephesians 6:1—Children, obey your parents in the Lord: for this is right.

Colossians 3:6—For which things' sake the wrath of God cometh on the children of disobedience.

1 Peter 2:13, 14—Submit yourselves to every ordinance of man for the Lord's sake: whether it be to the king, as supreme; Or unto governors, as unto them that are sent by him for the punishment of evil-doers, and for the praise of them that do well.

Dissatisfaction

Psalms 37:19—They shall not be ashamed in the evil time: and in the days of famine they shall be satisfied.

Psalms 63:5—My soul shall be satisfied as with marrow and fatness; and my mouth shall praise thee with joyful lips.

Psalms 91:16—With long life will I satisfy him, and shew him my salvation.

Psalms 107:8, 9—Oh that men would praise the Lord for his goodness, and for his wonderful works to the children of men! For he satisfieth the longing soul, and filleth the hungry soul with goodness.

Proverbs 19:23—The fear of the Lord tendeth to life: and he that hath it shall abide satisfied; he shall not be visited with evil.

Philippians 4:11—Not that I speak in respect of want: for I have learned, in whatsoever state I am, therewith to be content.

Drunkenness

Proverbs 23:21—For the drunkard and the glutton shall come to poverty: and drowsiness shall clothe a man with rags.

Isaiah 5:11—Woe unto them that rise up early in the morning, that they may follow strong drink; that continue until night, till wine inflame them!

Romans 13:13—Let us walk honestly, as in the day; not in rioting and drunkenness, not in chambering and wantonness, not in strife and envying.

30

1 Corinthians 6:10—Nor thieves, nor covetous, nor drunkards, nor revilers, nor extortioners, shall inherit the kingdom of God.

1 Thessalonians 5:7, 8—For they that sleep sleep in the night; and they that be drunken are drunken in the night. But let us, who are of the day, be sober, putting on the breastplate of faith and love; and for an helmet, the hope of salvation.

E

Endurance

Mark 13:13—And ye shall be hated of all men for my name's sake: but he that shall endure unto the end, the same shall be saved.

2 Timothy 2:3—Thou therefore endure hardness, as a good soldier of Jesus Christ.

Hebrews 12:7—If ye endure chastening, God dealeth with you as with sons; for what son is he whom the father chasteneth not?

James 1:12—Blessed is the man that endureth temptation: for when he is tried, he shall receive the crown of life, which the Lord hath promised to them that love him.

James 5:11—Behold, we count them happy which endure. Ye have heard of the patience of Job, and have seen the end of the Lord; that the Lord is very pitiful, and of tender mercy.

1 Peter 1:25—But the word of the Lord endureth for ever. And this is the word which by the gospel is preached unto you.

Enemies

Deuteronomy 28:7—The Lord shall cause thine enemies that rise up against thee to be smitten before thy face: they shall come out against thee one way, and flee before thee seven ways.

Psalms 18:47, 48—It is God that avengeth me, and subdueth the people under me. He delivereth me from mine enemies: yea, thou liftest me up above those that rise up against me: thou hast delivered me from the violent man.

Psalms 23:5—Thou preparest a table before me in the presence of mine enemies: thou anointest my head with oil; my cup runneth over.

Proverbs 16:7—When a man's ways please the Lord, he maketh even his enemies to be at peace with him.

Luke 6:27—But I say unto you which hear, Love your enemies, do good to them which hate you.

Luke 10:19—Behold, I give unto you power to tread on serpents and scorpions, and over all the power of the enemy: and nothing shall by any means hurt you.

Envy

Proverbs 14:30—A sound heart is the life of the flesh: but envy the rottenness of the bones.

Proverbs 23:17—Let not thine heart envy sinners: but be thou in the fear of the Lord all the day long.

1 Corinthians 13:4—Charity suffereth long, and is kind; charity envieth not; charity vaunteth not itself, is not puffed up.

Galatians 5:26—Let us not be desirous of vain glory, provoking one another, envying one another.

James 3:16—For where envying and strife is, there is confusion and every evil work.

1 Peter 2:1—Wherefore laying aside all malice, and all guile, and hypocrisies, and envies, and all evil speakings.

Evil

Psalms 91:10—There shall no evil befall thee, neither shall any plague come nigh thy dwelling.

Psalms 121:7—The Lord shall preserve thee from all evil: he shall preserve thy soul.

Proverbs 11:19—As righteousness tendeth to life: so he that pursueth evil pursueth it to his own death.

Proverbs 12:21—There shall no evil happen to the just: but the wicked shall be filled with mischief.

Ecclesiastes 8:5—Whoso keepeth the commandment shall feel no evil thing: and a wise man's heart discerneth both time and judgment.

Romans 12:21—Be not overcome of evil, but overcome evil with good.

Galatians 1:4—Who gave himself for our sins, that he might deliver us from this present evil world, according to the will of God and our Father.

Ephesians 5:15, 16—See then that ye walk circumspectly, not as fools, but as wise, Redeeming the time, because the days are evil.

1 Thessalonians 5:22—Abstain from all appearance of evil.

James 3:8—But the tongue can no man tame; it is an unruly evil, full of deadly poison.

F

Faith

Psalms 118:8—It is better to trust in the Lord than to put confidence in man.

Proverbs 3:26—For the Lord shall be thy confidence, and shall keep thy foot from being taken.

Isaiah 43:1, 2—But now thus saith the Lord that created thee, O Jacob, and he that formed thee, O Israel, Fear not: for I have redeemed thee, I have called thee by thy name; thou art mine. When thou passest through the waters, I will be with thee; and through the rivers, they shall not overflow thee: when thou walkest through the fire, thou shalt not be burned; neither shall the flame kindle upon thee.

Matthew 6:30—Wherefore, if God so clothe the grass of the field, which to day is, and to morrow is cast into the oven, shall he not much more clothe you, O ye of little faith?

Matthew 17:20—And Jesus said unto them, Because of your unbelief: for verily I say unto you, If ye have faith as a grain of mustard seed, ye shall say unto this mountain, Remove hence to yonder place; and it shall remove; and nothing shall be impossible unto you.

Romans 10:17—So then faith cometh by hearing, and hearing by the word of God.

Romans 12:3—For I say, through the grace given unto me, to every man that is among you, not to think of himself more highly than he ought to think; but to think soberly, according as God hath dealt to every man the measure of faith.

Romans 14:23—And he that doubteth is damned if he eat, because he eateth not of faith: for whatsoever is not of faith is sin.

2 Corinthians 5:7—For we walk by faith, not by sight.

Galatians 3:13, 14—Christ hath redeemed us from the curse of the law, being made a curse for us: for it is written, Cursed is every one that hangeth on a tree: That the blessing of Abraham might come on the

Gentiles through Jesus Christ; that we might receive the promise of the Spirit through faith.

Galatians 6:9—And let us not be weary in well doing: for in due season we shall reap, if we faint not.

Ephesians 6:12, 13—For we wrestle not against flesh and blood, but against principalities, against powers, against the rulers of the darkness of this world, against spiritual wickedness in high places. Wherefore take unto you the whole armour of God, that ye may be able to withstand in the evil day, and having done all, to stand.

Ephesians 6:16—Above all, taking the shield of faith, wherewith ye shall be able to quench all the fiery darts of the wicked.

1 Timothy 6:12—Fight the good fight of faith, lay hold on eternal life, whereunto thou art also called, and hast professed a good profession before many witnesses.

Hebrews 10:23—Let us hold fast the profession of our faith without wavering; (for he is faithful that promised).

Hebrews 10:38—Now the just shall live by faith: but if any man draw back, my soul shall have no pleasure in him.

Hebrews 11:6—But without faith it is impossible to please him: for he that cometh to God must believe that he is, and that he is a rewarder of them that diligently seek him.

Hebrews 12:2—Looking unto Jesus the author and finisher of our faith; who for the joy that was set before him endured the cross, despising the shame, and is set down at the right hand of the throne of God.

James 2:17—Even so faith, if it hath not works, is dead, being alone.

Fear

Psalms 3:3—But thou, O Lord, art a shield for me; my glory, and the lifter up of mine head.

Psalms 91:5—Thou shalt not be afraid for the terror by night; nor for the arrow that flieth by day.

Psalms 91:11—For he shall give his angels charge over thee, to keep thee in all thy ways.

Psalms 118:6—The Lord is on my side; I will not fear: what can man do unto me?

Proverbs 3:24—When thou liest down, thou shalt not be afraid: yea, thou shalt lie down, and thy sleep shall be sweet.

Proverbs 29:25—The fear of man bringeth a snare: but whoso putteth his trust in the Lord shall be safe.

Isaiah 54:14—In righteousness shalt thou be established: thou shalt be far from oppression; for thou shalt not fear: and from terror; for it shall not come near thee.

Matthew 10:28—And fear not them which kill the body, but are not able to kill the soul: but rather fear him which is able to destroy both soul and body in hell.

Romans 8:15—For ye have not received the spirit of bondage again to fear; but ye have received the Spirit of adoption, whereby we cry, Abba, Father.

Hebrews 13:6—So that we may boldly say, The Lord is my helper, and I will not fear what man shall do unto me.

1 Peter 3:14—But and if ye suffer for righteousness' sake, happy are ye: and be not afraid of their terror, neither be troubled.

1 John 4:18—There is no fear in love; but perfect love casteth out fear: because fear hath torment. He that feareth is not made perfect in love.

Flattery

Psalms 12:3—The Lord shall cut off all flattering lips, and the tongue that speaketh proud things.

Proverbs 20:19—He that goeth about as a talebearer revealeth secrets: therefore meddle not with him that flattereth with his lips.

Proverbs 26:28—A lying tongue hateth those that are afflicted by it; and a flattering mouth worketh ruin.

Proverbs 29:5—A man that flattereth his neighbour spreadeth a net for his feet.

Foolishness

Psalms 69:5—O God, thou knowest my foolishness; and my sins are not hid from thee.

Proverbs 12:23—A prudent man concealeth knowledge: but the heart of fools proclaimeth foolishness.

Proverbs 19:3—The foolishness of man perverteth his way: and his heart fretteth against the Lord.

Proverbs 22:15—Foolishness is bound in the heart of a child; but the rod of correction shall drive it far from him.

Proverbs 24:9—The thought of foolishness is sin: and the scorner is an abomination to men.

1 Corinthians 3:18, 19—Let no man deceive himself. If any man among you seemeth to be wise in this world, let him become a fool, that he may be wise. For the wisdom of this world is foolishness with God. For it is written, He taketh the wise in their own craftiness.

Forgiveness

Matthew 6:14—For if ye forgive men their trespasses, your heavenly Father will also forgive you.

Mark 3:29—But he that shall blaspheme against the Holy Ghost hath never forgiveness, but is in danger of eternal damnation.

Mark 11:25—And when ye stand praying, forgive, if ye have ought against any: that your Father also which is in heaven may forgive you your trespasses.

Ephesians 4:32—And be ye kind one to another, tender-hearted, forgiving one another, even as God for Christ's sake hath forgiven you.

James 5:15—And the prayer of faith shall save the sick, and the Lord shall raise him up; and if he have committed sins, they shall be forgiven him.

1 John 1:9—If we confess our sins, he is faithful and just to forgive us our sins, and to cleanse us from all un-righteousness.

Fornication

1 Corinthians 6:18—Flee fornication. Every sin that a man doeth is without the body; but he that committeth fornication sinneth against his own body.

1 Corinthians 7:2—Nevertheless, to avoid fornication, let every man have his own wife, and let every woman have her own husband.

1 Corinthians 10:8—Neither let us commit fornication, as some of them committed, and fell in one day three and twenty thousand.

Galatians 5:19—How the works of the flesh are manifest, which are these; Adultery, fornication, uncleanness, lasciviousness.

1 Thessalonians 4:3, 4—For this is the will of God, even your sanctification, that ye should abstain from fornication: That every one of you should know how to possess his vessel in sanctification and honour.

G

Giving

Proverbs 19:17—He that hath pity upon the poor lendeth unto the Lord; and that which he hath given will he pay him again.

Ecclesiastes 11:1—Cast thy bread upon the waters: for thou shalt find it after many days.

Luke 6:38—Give, and it shall be given unto you; good measure, pressed down, and shaken together, and running over, shall men give into your bosom. For with the same measure that ye mete withal it shall be measured to you again.

2 Corinthians 9:6—But this I say, He which soweth sparingly shall reap also sparingly; and he which soweth bountifully shall reap also bountifully.

Grief

Psalms 126:5—They that sow in tears shall reap in joy.

Isaiah 53:3, 4—He is despised and rejected of men; a man of sorrows, and acquainted with grief: and we hid as it were our faces from him; he was despised and we esteemed him not. Surely he hath borne our griefs, and carried our sorrows: yet we did esteem him stricken, smitten of God, and afflicted.

Lamentations 3:31–33—For the Lord will not cast off for ever: But though he cause grief, yet will he have compassion according to the multitude of his mercies. For he doth not afflict willingly nor grieve the children of men.

Matthew 5:4—Blessed are they that mourn: for they shall be comforted.

1 Peter 2:19—For this is thankworthy, if a man for conscience toward God endure grief, suffering wrongfully.

Guidance

Psalms 48:14—For this God is our God for ever and ever: he will be our guide even unto death.

Psalms 73:24—Thou shalt guide me with thy counsel, and afterward receive me to glory.

Psalms 119:105—Thy word is a lamp unto my feet, and a light unto my path.

Proverbs 3:6—In all thy ways acknowledge him, and he shall direct thy paths.

Proverbs 11:3—The integrity of the upright shall guide them: but the perverseness of transgressors shall destroy them.

Proverbs 16:9—A man's heart deviseth his way: but the Lord directeth his steps.

Isaiah 58:11—And the Lord shall guide thee continually, and satisfy thy soul in drought, and make fat thy bones: and thou shalt be like a watered garden, and like a spring of water, whose waters fail not.

John 16:13—Howbeit when he, the Spirit of truth, is come, he will guide you into all truth: for he shall not speak of himself; but whatsoever he shall hear, that shall he speak: and he will shew you things to come.

H

Hatred

Proverbs 10:12—Hatred stirreth up strifes: but love covereth all sins.

Matthew 5:44—But I say unto you, Love your enemies, bless them that curse you, do good to them that hate you, and pray for them which despitefully use you, and persecute you.

John 15:12—This is my commandment, That ye love one another, as I have loved you.

John 15:18—If the world hate you, ye know that it hated me before it hated you.

1 Corinthians 13:3—And though I bestow all my goods to feed the poor, and though I give my body to be burned, and have not charity, it profiteth me nothing.

Hebrews 10:24—And let us consider one another to provoke unto love and to good works.

1 Peter 1:22—Seeing ye have purified your souls in obeying the truth through the Spirit unto unfeigned love of the brethren, see that ye love one another with a pure heart fervently.

1 John 2:10—He that loveth his brother abideth in the light, and there is none occasion of stumbling in him.

1 John 3:14—We know that we have passed from death unto life, because we love the brethren. He that loveth not his brother abideth in death.

1 John 3:18—My little children, let us not love in word, neither in tongue; but in deed and in truth.

1 John 3:23—And this is his commandment, That we should believe on the name of his Son Jesus Christ, and love one another as he gave us commandment.

1 John 4:8—He that loveth not knoweth not God; for God is love.

1 John 4:12—No man hath seen God at any time. If we love one another, God dwelleth in us, and his love is perfected in us.

Help

Psalms 33:20—Our soul waiteth for the Lord: he is our help and our shield.

Psalms 40:17—But I am poor and needy; yet the Lord thinketh upon me: thou art my help and my deliverer; make no tarrying, O my God.

Psalms 46:1—God is our refuge and strength, a very present help in trouble.

Psalms 54:4—Behold, God is mine helper: the Lord is with them that uphold my soul.

Psalms 121:1, 2—I will lift up mine eyes unto the hills, from whence cometh my help. My help cometh from the Lord, which made heaven and earth.

Psalms 124:8—Our help is in the name of the Lord, who made heaven and earth.

Isaiah 41:10—Fear thou not; for I am with thee: be not dismayed; for I am thy God: I will strengthen thee; yea, I will help thee; yea, I will uphold thee with the right hand of my righteousness.

Heresy

Galatians 5:20, 21—Idolatry, witchcraft, hatred, variance, emulations, wrath, strife, seditions, heresies, Envyings, murders, drunkenness, revellings, and such like: of the which I tell you before, as I have also told you in time past, that they which do such things shall not inherit the kingdom of God.

2 Peter 2:1—But there were false prophets also among the people, even as there shall be false teachers among you, who privily shall bring in damnable

51

heresies, even denying the Lord that bought them, and bring upon themselves swift destruction.

2 John 9, 10—Whosoever transgresseth, and abideth not in the doctrine of Christ, hath not God. He that abideth in the doctrine of Christ, he hath both the Father and the Son. If there come any unto you, and bring not this doctrine, receive him not into your house, neither bid him God speed.

Holiness

Romans 6:19—I speak after the manner of men because of the infirmity of your flesh: for as ye have yielded your members servants to uncleanness and to iniquity unto iniquity; even so now yield your members servants to righteousness unto holiness.

2 Corinthians 7:1—Having therefore these promises, dearly beloved, let us cleanse ourselves from all filthiness of the flesh and spirit, perfecting holiness in the fear of God.

Ephesians 4:24—And that ye put on the new man, which after God is created in righteousness and true holiness.

1 Thessalonians 4:7—For God hath not called us unto uncleanness, but unto holiness.

2 Timothy 2:21—If a man therefore purge himself from these, he shall be a vessel unto honour, sanctified, and meet for the master's use, and prepared unto every good work.

Hebrews 12:10—For they verily for a few days chastened us after their own pleasure; but he for our profit, that we might be partakers of his holiness.

Hopelessness

Psalms 33:18, 19—Behold, the eye of the Lord is upon them that fear him, upon them that hope in his mercy; To deliver their soul from death, and to keep them alive in famine.

Psalms 37:4—Delight thyself also in the Lord; and he shall give thee the desires of thine heart.

Psalms 42:11—Why art thou cast down, O my soul? and why art thou disquieted within me? hope thou in God: for I shall yet praise him, who is the health of my countenance, and my God.

Psalms 146:5—Happy is he that hath the God of Jacob for his help, whose hope is in the Lord his God.

Romans 8:25—But if we hope for that we see not, then do we with patience wait for it.

Romans 15:13—Now the God of hope fill you with all joy and peace in believing, that ye may abound in hope, through the power of the Holy Ghost.

Ephesians 1:18—The eyes of your understanding being enlightened; that ye may know what is the hope of his calling, and what the riches of the glory of his inheritance in the saints.

Humility

2 Chronicles 7:14—If my people, which are called by my name, shall humble themselves, and pray, and seek my face, and turn from their wicked ways; then will I hear from heaven, and will forgive their sin, and will heal their land.

Proverbs 22:4—By humility and the fear of the Lord are riches, and honour, and life.

Proverbs 29:23—A man's pride shall bring him low: but honour shall uphold the humble in spirit.

Matthew 18:4—Whosoever therefore shall humble himself as this little child, the same is greatest in the kingdom of heaven.

James 4:10—Humble yourselves in the sight of the Lord, and he shall lift you up.

1 Peter 5:6—Humble yourselves therefore under the mighty hand of God, that he may exalt you in due time.

Hypocrisy

Job 13:16—He also shall be my salvation: for an hypocrite shall not come before him.

Proverbs 11:9—An hypocrite with his mouth destroyeth his neighbour: but through knowledge shall the just be delivered.

Isaiah 32:6—For the vile person will speak villany, and his heart will work iniquity, to practise hypocrisy, and to utter error against the Lord, to make empty the soul of the hungry, and he will cause the drink of the thirsty to fail.

Matthew 7:3-5—And why beholdest thou the mote that is in thy brother's eye, but considerest not the beam that is in thine own eye? Or how wilt thou say to thy brother, Let me pull out the mote out of thine eye; and, behold, a beam is in thine own eye? Thou hypocrite, first cast out the beam out of thine own eye;

and then shalt thou see clearly to cast out the mote out of thy brother's eye.

Luke 12:1, 2—In the mean time, when there were gathered together an innumerable multitude of people, insomuch that they trode one upon another, he began to say unto his disciples first of all, Beware ye of the leaven of the Pharisees, which is hypocrisy. For there is nothing covered, that shall not be revealed; neither hid, that shall not be known.

1 Timothy 4:1, 2—Now the Spirit speaketh expressly, that in the latter times some shall depart from the faith, giving heed to seducing spirits, and doctrines of devils; Speaking lies in hypocrisy; having their conscience seared with a hot iron.

James 3:17—But the wisdom that is from above is first pure, then peaceable, gentle, and easy to be intreated, full of mercy and good fruits, without partiality, and without hypocrisy.

I

Idolatry

Exodus 20:3—Thou shalt have no other gods before me.

1 Corinthians 6:9—Know ye not that the unrighteous shall not inherit the kingdom of God? Be not deceived: neither fornicators, nor idolators, nor adulterers, nor effeminate, nor abusers of themselves with mankind.

1 Corinthians 10:14—Wherefore, my dearly beloved, flee from idolatry.

1 John 5:21—Little children, keep yourselves from idols. Amen.

Revelation 21:8—But the fearful, and unbelieving, and the abominable, and murderers, and whore-mongers, and sorcerers, and idolaters, and all liars, shall have their part in the lake which burneth with fire and brimstone: which is the second death.

Impatience

Psalms 27:14—Wait on the Lord: be of good courage, and he shall strengthen thine heart: wait, I say, on the Lord.

Psalms 37:9—For evildoers shall be cut off: but those that wait upon the Lord, they shall inherit the earth.

Isaiah 40:31—But they that wait upon the Lord shall renew their strength; they shall mount up with wings as eagles; they shall run, and not be weary; and they shall walk, and not faint.

Luke 8:15—But that on the good ground are they, which in an honest and good heart, having heard the word, keep it, and bring forth fruit with patience.

Luke 21:19—In your patience possess ye your souls.

Romans 15:4—For whatsoever things were written aforetime were written for our learning, that we through patience and comfort of the scriptures might have hope.

Hebrews 6:12—That ye be not slothful, but followers of them who through faith and patience inherit the promises.

James 1:4—But let patience have her perfect work, that ye may be perfect and entire, wanting nothing.

James 5:8—Be ye also patient; stablish your hearts: for the coming of the Lord draweth nigh.

Imperfection

Psalms 138:8—The Lord will perfect that which concerneth me: thy mercy, O Lord, endureth for ever: forsake not the works of thine own hands.

John 17:22, 23—And the glory which thou gavest me I have given them; that they may be one, even as we are one: I in them, and thou in me, that they may be made perfect in one; and that the world may know that thou hast sent me, and hast loved them, as thou hast loved me.

Colossians 1:28—Whom we preach, warning every man, and teaching every man in all wisdom; that we may present every man perfect in Christ Jesus.

Colossians 3:14—And above all these things put on charity, which is the bond of perfectness.

Hebrews 7:19—For the law made nothing perfect, but the bringing in of a better hope did; by the which we draw nigh unto God.

James 3:2—For in many things we offend all. If any man offend not in word, the same is a perfect man, and able also to bridle the whole body.

1 Peter 5:10—But the God of all grace, who hath called us unto his eternal glory by Christ Jesus, after that ye have suffered a while, make you perfect, stablish, strengthen, settle you.

Indiscretion

Proverbs 2:11—Discretion shall preserve thee, understanding shall keep thee.

Proverbs 3:21—My son, let not them depart from thine eyes: keep sound wisdom and discretion.

Proverbs 11:22—As a jewel of gold in a swine's snout, so is a fair woman which is without discretion.

Proverbs 19:11—The discretion of a man deferreth his anger; and it is his glory to pass over a transgression.

Inferiority

Genesis 1:26—And God said, Let us make man in our image, after our likeness: and let them have dominion over the fish of the sea, and over the fowl of the air, and over the cattle, and over all the earth, and over every creeping thing that creepeth upon the earth.

Matthew 5:48—Be ye therefore perfect, even as your Father which is in heaven is perfect.

2 Corinthians 5:21—For he hath made him to be sin for us, who knew no sin; that we might be made the righteousness of God in him.

Colossians 2:10—And ye are complete in him, which is the head of all principality and power.

1 Peter 1:23—Being born again, not of corruptible seed, but of incorruptible, by the word of God, which liveth and abideth for ever.

1 Peter 2:9—But ye are a chosen generation, a royal priesthood, an holy nation, a peculiar people; that ye should shew forth the praises of him who hath called you out of darkness into his marvellous light.

2 Peter 1:3—According as his divine power hath given unto us all things that pertain unto life and godliness, through the knowledge of him that hath called us to glory and virtue.

1 John 4:17—Herein is our love made perfect, that we may have boldness in the day of judgment: because as he is, so are we in this world.

Revelation 1:6—And hath made us kings and priests unto God and his Father; to him be glory and dominion for ever and ever. Amen.

Inhospitality

Romans 12:20—Therefore if thine enemy hunger, feed him; if he thirst, give him drink: for in so doing thou shalt heap coals of fire on his head.

Titus 1:7, 8—For a bishop must be blameless, as the steward of God; not selfwilled, not soon angry, not given to wine, no striker, not given to filthy lucre; But a lover of hospitality, a lover of good men, sober, just, holy, temperate.

Hebrews 13:2—Be not forgetful to entertain strangers: for thereby some have entertained angels unaware.

1 Peter 4:9—Use hospitality one to another without grudging.

Intemperance

1 Corinthians 9:25—And every man that striveth for the mastery is temperate in all things. Now they do it to obtain a corruptible crown; but we an incorruptible.

Galatians 5:22, 23—But the fruit of the Spirit is love, joy, peace, longsuffering, gentleness, goodness, faith, Meekness, temperance: against such there is no law.

Philippians 4:5—Let your moderation be known unto all men. The Lord is at hand.

2 Peter 1:5, 6—And beside this, giving all diligence, add to your faith virtue; and to virtue knowledge; And to knowledge temperance; and to temperance patience; and to patience godliness.

J

Judging

Psalms 50:6—And the heavens shall declare his righteousness: for God is judge himself.

Ecclesiastes 3:17—I said in mine heart, God shall judge the righteous and the wicked: for there is a time there for every purpose and for every work.

Matthew 7:1, 2—Judge not, that ye be not judged. For with what judgment ye judge, ye shall be judged:

and with what measure ye mete, it shall be measured to you again.

Romans 14:13—Let us not therefore judge one another any more: but judge this rather, that no man put a stumblingblock or an occasion to fall in his brother's way.

Colossians 2:16—Let no man therefore judge you in meat, or in drink, or in respect of an holyday, or of the new moon, or of the sabbath days.

1 Peter 4:17—For the time is come that judgment must begin at the house of God: and if it first begin at us, what shall the end be of them that obey not the gospel of God?

Justification

Isaiah 43:26—Put me in remembrance: let us plead together: declare thou, that thou mayest be justified.

Matthew 12:37—For by thy words thou shalt be justified, and by thy words thou shalt be condemned.

Romans 2:13—For not the hearers of the law are just before God, but the doers of the law shall be justified.

Romans 5:9—Much more then, being now justified by his blood, we shall be saved from wrath through him.

1 Corinthians 6:11—And such were some of you: but ye are washed, but ye are sanctified, but ye are justified in the name of the Lord Jesus, and by the Spirit of our God.

Galatians 2:16—Knowing that a man is not justified by the works of the law, but by the faith of Jesus Christ, even we have believed in Jesus Christ, that we might be justified by the faith of Christ, and not by the works of the law: for by the works of the law shall no flesh be justified.

K

Killing

Exodus 20:13—Thou shalt not kill.

Proverbs 6:16, 17—These six things doth the Lord hate:
yea, seven are an abomination unto him: A proud
look, a lying tongue, and hands that shed innocent
blood.

Matthew 5:21, 22—Ye have heard that it was said by
them of old time, Thou shalt not kill; and whoso-

ever shall kill shall be in danger of the judgment:
But I say unto you, That whosoever is angry with
his brother without a cause shall be in danger of the
judgment: and whosoever shall say to his brother,
Raca, shall be in danger of the council: but whosoever shall say, Thou fool, shall be in danger of hell
fire.

Matthew 10:28—And fear not them which kill the body,
but are not able to kill the soul: but rather fear him
which is able to destroy both soul and body in hell.

John 10:10—The thief cometh not, but for to steal, and
to kill, and to destroy: I am come that they might
have life, and that they might have it more abundantly.

Galatians 5:21—Envyings, murders, drunkenness, revellings, and such like: of the which I tell you before,
as I have also told you in time past, that they which
do such things shall not inherit the kingdom of
God.

1 John 3:15—Whosoever hateth his brother is a murderer: and ye know that no murderer hath eternal
life abiding in him.

Knowledge

Proverbs 2:6—For the Lord giveth wisdom: out of his
mouth cometh knowledge and understanding.

Hosea 4:6—My people are destroyed for lack of knowledge: because thou hast rejected knowledge, I will
also reject thee, that thou shalt be no priest to me:
seeing thou hast forgotten the law of thy God, I will
also forget thy children.

Romans 11:33—O the depth of the riches both of the wisdom and knowledge of God! how unsearchable are his judgments, and his ways past finding out!

1 Corinthians 1:30—But of him are ye in Christ Jesus, who of God is made unto us wisdom, and righteousness, and sanctification, and redemption.

James 1:5—If any of you lack wisdom, let him ask of God, that giveth to all men liberally, and upbraideth not; and it shall be given him.

2 Peter 1:2—Grace and peace be multiplied unto you through the knowledge of God, and of Jesus our Lord.

L

Laziness

Proverbs 10:4—He becometh poor that dealeth with a slack hand: but the hand of the diligent maketh rich.

Proverbs 12:24—The hand of the diligent shall bear rule: but the slothful shall be under tribute.

Proverbs 15:19—The way of the slothful man is as an hedge of thorns: but the way of the righteous is made plain.

Proverbs 18:9—He also that is slothful in his work is brother to him that is a great waster.

Proverbs 21:25—The desire of the slothful killeth him; for his hands refuse to labour.

Ecclesiastes 9:10—Whatsoever thy hand findeth to do, do it with thy might; for there is no work, nor device, nor knowledge, nor wisdom, in the grave, whither thou goest.

Romans 12:11—Not slothful in business; fervent in spirit; serving the Lord.

1 Corinthians 3:9—For we are labourers together with God: ye are God's husbandry, ye are God's building.

Loneliness

Psalms 9:10—And they that know thy name will put their trust in thee: for thou, Lord, hast not forsaken them that seek thee.

Psalms 34:22—The Lord redeemeth the soul of his servants: and none of them that trust in him shall be desolate.

John 14:16—And I will pray the Father, and he shall give you another Comforter, that he may abide with you for ever.

Hebrews 13:5—Let your conversation be without covetousness; and be content with such things as ye have: for he hath said, I will never leave thee, nor forsake thee.

Lust

Mark 4:18, 19—And these are they which are sown among thorns; such as hear the word, And the cares of this world, and the deceitfulness of riches, and the lusts of other things entering in, choke the word, and it becometh unfruitful.

Romans 8:13—For if ye live after the flesh, ye shall die: but if ye through the Spirit do mortify the deeds of the body, ye shall live.

1 Corinthians 10:6—Now these things were our examples, to the intent we should not lust after evil things, as they also lusted.

Galatians 5:16—This I say then, Walk in the Spirit, and ye shall not fulfil the lust of the flesh.

Galatians 5:24—And they that are Christ's have crucified the flesh with the affections and lusts.

1 John 2:16, 17—For all that is in the world, the lust of the flesh, and the lust of the eyes, and the pride of life, is not of the Father, but is of the world. And the world passeth away, and the lust thereof: but he that doeth the will of God abideth for ever.

Lying

Psalms 31:18—Let the lying lips be put to silence; which speak grievous things proudly and contemptuously against the righteous.

Psalms 101:7—He that worketh deceit shall not dwell within my house: he that telleth lies shall not tarry in my sight.

Psalms 120:2—Deliver my soul, O Lord, from lying lips, and from a deceitful tongue.

Proverbs 12:22—Lying lips are abomination to the Lord: but they that deal truly are his delight.

Proverbs 19:5—A false witness shall not be unpunished, and he that speaketh lies shall not escape.

Revelation 21:8—But the fearful, and unbelieving, and the abominable, and murderers, and whoremongers, and sorcerers, and idolaters, and all liars, shall have their part in the lake which burneth with fire and brimstone: which is the second death.

M

Marriage

1 Corinthians 7:3—Let the husband render unto the wife due benevolence: and likewise also the wife unto the husband.

1 Corinthians 7:14—For the unbelieving husband is sanctified by the wife, and the unbelieving wife is sanctified by the husband: else were your children unclean; but now are they holy.

Ephesians 5:25—Husbands, love your wives, even as Christ also loved the church, and gave himself for it.

Ephesians 6:4—And, ye fathers, provoke not your children to wrath: but bring them up in the nurture and admonition of the Lord.

1 Peter 3:1—Likewise, ye wives, be in subjection to your own husbands; that, if any obey not the word, they also may without the word be won by the conversation of the wives.

1 Peter 3:7—Likewise, ye husbands, dwell with them according to knowledge, giving honour unto the wife, as unto the weaker vessel, and as being heirs together of the grace of life; that your prayers be not hindered.

Meekness

Psalms 22:26—The meek shall eat and be satisfied: they shall praise the Lord that seek him: your heart shall live for ever.

Psalms 25:9—The meek will he guide in judgment: and the meek will he teach his way.

Psalms 37:11—But the meek shall inherit the earth; and shall delight themselves in the abundance of peace.

Psalms 147:6—The Lord lifteth up the meek: he casteth the wicked down to the ground.

Psalms 149:4—For the Lord taketh pleasure in his people: he will beautify the meek with salvation.

Matthew 5:5—Blessed are the meek: for they shall inherit the earth.

Titus 3:2—To speak evil of no man, to be no brawlers, but gentle, shewing all meekness unto all men.

1 Peter 3:4—But let it be the hidden man of the heart, in that which is not corruptible, even the ornament of a meek and quiet spirit, which is in the sight of God of great price.

Mercy

Psalms 23:6—Surely goodness and mercy shall follow me all the days of my life: and I will dwell in the house of the Lord for ever.

Proverbs 3:3—Let not mercy and truth forsake thee: bind them about thy neck; write them upon the table of thine heart.

Proverbs 11:17—The merciful man doeth good to his own soul: but he that is cruel troubleth his own flesh.

Proverbs 14:21—He that despiseth his neighbour sinneth: but he that hath mercy on the poor, happy is he.

Matthew 5:7—Blessed are the merciful: for they shall obtain mercy.

Luke 6:36—Be ye therefore merciful, as your Father also is merciful.

Mind

Proverbs 10:7—The memory of the just is blessed: but the name of the wicked shall rot.

Romans 12:2—And be not conformed to this world: but be ye transformed by the renewing of your mind, that ye may prove what is that good, and acceptable, and perfect, will of God.

1 Corinthians 2:16—For who hath known the mind of the Lord, that he may instruct him? But we have the mind of Christ.

2 Corinthians 10:5—Casting down imaginations, and every high thing that exalteth itself against the knowledge of God, and bringing into captivity every thought to the obedience of Christ.

Philippians 2:5-7—Let this mind be in you, which was also in Christ Jesus: Who, being in the form of God, thought it not robbery to be equal with God: But made himself of no reputation, and took upon him the form of a servant, and was made in the likeness of men.

Philippians 4:7—And the peace of God, which passeth all understanding, shall keep your hearts and minds through Christ Jesus.

2 Timothy 1:7—For God hath not given us the spirit of fear; but of power, and of love, and of a sound mind.

James 1:8—A double minded man is unstable in all his ways.

Money

Exodus 22:25—If thou lend money to any of my people that is poor by thee, thou shalt not be to him as an usurer, neither shalt thou lay upon him usury.

Isaiah 55:1, 2—Ho, every one that thirsteth, come ye to the waters, and he that hath no money; come ye, buy, and eat; yea, come, buy wine and milk without money and without price. Wherefore do ye spend money for that which is not bread? and your labour for that which satisfieth not? hearken diligently unto me, and eat ye that which is good, and let your soul delight itself in fatness.

1 Timothy 6:10—For the love of money is the root of all evil: which while some coveted after, they have erred from the faith, and pierced themselves through with many sorrows.

N

Need

Matthew 6:31, 32—Therefore take no thought, saying, What shall we eat? or, What shall we drink? or, Wherewithal shall we be clothed? (For after all these things do the Gentiles seek:) for your heavenly Father knoweth that ye have need of all these things.

Luke 12:32—Fear not, little flock; for it is your Father's good pleasure to give you the kingdom.

Romans 8:32—He that spared not his own Son, but delivered him up for us all, how shall he not with him also freely give us all things?

Philippians 4:19—But my God shall supply all your need according to his riches in glory by Christ Jesus.

Hebrews 4:16—Let us therefore come boldly unto the throne of grace, that we may obtain mercy, and find grace to help in time of need.

Neighbors

Exodus 20:16, 17—Thou shalt not bear false witness against thy neighbour. Thou shalt not covet thy neighbour's house, thou shalt not covet thy neighbor's wife, nor his manservant, nor his maidservant, nor his ox, nor his ass, nor any thing that is thy neighbour's.

Leviticus 19:13—Thou shalt not defraud thy neighbour, neither rob him: the wages of him that is hired shall not abide with thee all night until the morning.

Leviticus 19:18—Thou shalt not avenge, nor bear any grudge against the children of thy people, but thou shalt love thy neighbour as thyself: I am the Lord.

Proverbs 11:12—He that is void of wisdom despiseth his neighbour: but a man of understanding holdeth his peace.

Proverbs 14:21—He that despiseth his neighbour sinneth: but he that hath mercy on the poor, happy is he.

Proverbs 24:28—Be not a witness against thy neighbour without cause; and deceive not with thy lips.

Proverbs 29:5—A man that flattereth his neighbour spreadeth a net for his feet.

Romans 15:2—Let every one of us please his neighbour for his good to edification.

Noise

Psalms 65:7—Which stilleth the noise of the seas, the noise of their waves, and the tumult of the people.

Psalms 66:1—Make a joyful noise unto God, all ye lands.

Psalms 93:4—The Lord on high is mightier than the noise of many waters, yea, than the mighty waves of the sea.

Isaiah 25:5—Thou shalt bring down the noise of strangers, as the heat in a dry place; even the heat with the shadow of a cloud: the branch of the terrible ones shall be brought low.

O

Obedience

Deuteronomy 11:26, 27—Behold, I set before you this
day a blessing and a curse; A blessing, if ye obey the
commandments of the Lord your God, which I
command you this day.

1 Samuel 15:22—And Samuel said, Hath the Lord as
great delight in burnt offerings and sacrifices, as in
obeying the voice of the Lord? Behold, to obey is

better than sacrifice, and to hearken than the fat of rams.

Proverbs 22:5—Thorns and snares are in the way of the froward: he that doth keep his soul shall be far from them.

Isaiah 1:19, 20—If ye be willing and obedient, ye shall eat the good of the land: But if ye refuse and rebel, ye shall be devoured with the sword: for the mouth of the Lord hath spoken it.

Acts 5:29—Then Peter and the other apostles answered and said, We ought to obey God rather than men.

Romans 6:16—Know ye not, that to whom ye yield yourselves servants to obey, his servants ye are to whom ye obey; whether of sin unto death, or of obedience unto righteousness?

Romans 12:1—I beseech you therefore, brethren, by the mercies of God, that ye present your bodies a living sacrifice, holy, acceptable unto God, which is your reasonable service.

Romans 13:1, 2—Let every soul be subject unto the higher powers. For there is no power but of God: the powers that be are ordained of God. Whosoever therefore resisteth the power, resisteth the ordinance of God: and they that resist shall receive to themselves damnation.

Oppression

Psalms 103:6—The Lord executeth righteousness and judgment for all that are oppressed.

Psalms 119:134—Deliver me from the oppression of man: so will I keep thy precepts.

Isaiah 54:14—In righteousness shalt thou be established: thou shalt be far from oppression; for thou shalt not fear: and from terror; for it shall not come near thee.

P

Persecution

Matthew 5:10—Blessed are they which are persecuted for righteousness' sake: for theirs is the kingdom of heaven.

Mark 4:16, 17—And these are they likewise which are sown on stony ground; who, when they have heard the word, immediately receive it with gladness; And have no root in themselves, and so endure but for a time: afterward, when affliction or persecution ariseth for the word's sake, immediately they are offended.

Romans 12:14—Bless them which persecute you: bless, and curse not.

2 Timothy 3:12—Yea, and all that will live godly in Christ Jesus shall suffer persecution.

Poverty

Joshua 1:8—This book of the law shall not depart out of thy mouth; but thou shalt meditate therein day and night, that thou mayest observe to do according to all that is written therein: for then thou shalt make thy way prosperous, and then thou shalt have good success.

Psalms 1:3—And he shall be like a tree planted by the rivers of water, that bringeth forth his fruit in his season; his leaf also shall not wither; and whatsoever he doeth shall prosper.

Psalms 23:1—The Lord is my shepherd; I shall not want.

Psalms 35:27—Let them shout for joy, and be glad, that favour my righteous cause: yea, let them say continually, Let the Lord be magnified, which hath pleasure in the prosperity of his servant.

Psalms 122:6—Pray for the peace of Jerusalem: they shall prosper that love thee.

Proverbs 13:22—A good man leaveth an inheritance to his children's children: and the wealth of the sinner is laid up for the just.

Proverbs 28:27—He that giveth unto the poor shall not lack: but he that hideth his eyes shall have many a curse.

Luke 6:38—Give, and it shall be given unto you; good measure, pressed down, and shaken together, and running over, shall men give into your bosom. For with the same measure that ye mete withal it shall be measured to you again.

2 Corinthians 8:9—For ye know the grace of our Lord Jesus Christ, that, though he was rich, yet for your sakes he became poor, that ye through his poverty might be rich.

3 John 2—Beloved, I wish above all things that thou mayest prosper and be in health, even as thy soul prospereth.

Praise

Psalms 42:5—Why art thou cast down, O my soul? and why art thou disquieted in me? hope thou in God: for I shall yet praise him for the help of his countenance.

Psalms 63:3, 4—Because thy lovingkindness is better than life, my lips shall praise thee. Thus will I bless thee while I live: I will lift up my hands in thy name.

Psalms 74:21—O let not the oppressed return ashamed: let the poor and needy praise thy name.

Psalms 107:31, 32—Oh that men would praise the Lord for his goodness, and for his wonderful works to the children of men! Let them exalt him also in the congregation of the people, and praise him in the assembly of the elders.

Psalms 135:3—Praise the Lord; for the Lord is good: sing praises unto his name; for it is pleasant.

Psalms 150:4—Praise him with the timbrel and dance: praise him with stringed instruments and organs.

1 Corinthians 6:20—For ye are bought with a price: therefore glorify God in your body, and in your spirit, which are God's.

Hebrews 13:15—By him therefore let us offer the sacrifice of praise to God continually, that is, the fruit of our lips giving thanks to his name.

Prayer

Matthew 6:6—But thou, when thou prayest, enter into thy closet, and when thou hast shut thy door, pray to thy Father which is in secret; and thy Father which seeth in secret shall reward thee openly.

Luke 18:1—And he spake a parable unto them to this end, that men ought always to pray, and not to faint.

Romans 8:26—Likewise the Spirit also helpeth our infirmities: for we know not what we should pray for as we ought: but the Spirit itself maketh intercession for us with groanings which cannot be uttered.

Ephesians 6:18—Praying always with all prayer and supplication in the Spirit, and watching thereunto with all perseverance and supplication for all saints.

Philippians 4:6—Be careful for nothing; but in every thing by prayer and supplication with thanksgiving let your requests be made known unto God.

Colossians 4:2—Continue in prayer, and watch in the same with thanksgiving.

James 5:16—Confess your faults one to another, and pray one for another, that ye may be healed. The effectual fervent prayer of a righteous man availeth much.

1 Peter 3:12—For the eyes of the Lord are over the righteous, and his ears are open unto their prayers: but the face of the Lord is against them that do evil.

Prejudice

Romans 3:22—Even the righteousness of God which is by faith of Jesus Christ unto all and upon all them that believe: for there is no difference.

Galatians 3:28—There is neither Jew nor Greek, there is neither bond nor free, there is neither male nor female: for ye are all one in Christ Jesus.

Colossians 3:11—Where there is neither Greek nor Jew, circumcision nor uncircumcision, Barbarian, Scythian, bond nor free: but Christ is all, and in all.

Pride

Psalms 37:11—But the meek shall inherit the earth; and shall delight themselves in the abundance of peace.

Proverbs 11:2—When pride cometh, then cometh shame: but with the lowly is wisdom.

Proverbs 13:10—Only by pride cometh contention: but with the well advised is wisdom.

Proverbs 16:18—Pride goeth before destruction, and an haughty spirit before a fall.

1 Peter 5:6—Humble yourselves therefore under the mighty hand of God, that he may exalt you in due time.

Q

Quenching

Song of Solomon 8:7—Many waters cannot quénch love, neither can the floods drown it: if a man would give all the substance of his house for love, it would utterly be contemned.

Ephesians 6:16—Above all, taking the shield of faith, wherewith ye shall be able to quench all the fiery darts of the wicked.

1 Thessalonians 5:19—Quench not the Spirit.

Quietness

Proverbs 1:33—But whoso hearkeneth unto me shall dwell safely, and shall be quiet from fear of evil.

Isaiah 32:17, 18—And the work of righteousness shall be peace; and the effect of righteousness quietness and assurance for ever. And my people shall dwell in a peaceable habitation, and in sure dwellings, and in quiet resting places.

1 Timothy 2:1, 2—I exhort therefore, that, first of all, supplications, prayers, intercessions, and giving of thanks, be made for all men; For kings, and for all that are in authority; that we may lead a quiet and peaceable life in all godliness and honesty.

R

Refuge

Psalms 46:11—The Lord of hosts is with us; the God of Jacob is our refuge.

Psalms 57:1—Be merciful unto me, O God, be merciful unto me: for my soul trusteth in thee: yea, in the shadow of thy wings will I make my refuge, until these calamities be overpast.

Psalms 62:8—Trust in him at all times; ye people, pour out your heart before him: God is a refuge for us.

Psalms 71:7—I am as a wonder unto many; but thou art my strong refuge.

Isaiah 25:4—For thou hast been a strength to the poor, a strength to the needy in his distress, a refuge from the storm, a shadow from the heat, when the blast of the terrible ones is as a storm against the wall.

Renewal

2 Corinthians 4:16—For which cause we faint not; but though our outward man perish, yet the inward man is renewed day by day.

Ephesians 4:23—And be renewed in the spirit of your mind.

Colossians 3:9, 10—Lie not one to another, seeing that ye have put off the old man with his deeds; And have put on the new man, which is renewed in knowledge after the image of him that created him.

Robbery

Exodus 20:15—Thou shalt not steal.

Proverbs 21:7—The robbery of the wicked shall destroy them; because they refuse to do judgment.

Ephesians 4:28—Let him that stole steal no more: but rather let him labour, working with his hands the thing which is good, that he may have to give to him that needeth.

S

Satan

Ephesians 4:27—Neither give place to the devil.

Ephesians 6:11—Put on the whole armour of God, that ye may be able to stand against the wiles of the devil.

Hebrews 2:14, 15—Forasmuch then as the children are partakers of flesh and blood, he also himself likewise took part of the same; that through death he might destroy him that had the power of death, that is, the devil; And deliver them who through fear of death were all their lifetime subject to bondage.

James 4:7—Submit yourselves therefore to God. Resist the devil, and he will flee from you.

1 Peter 5:8—Be sober, be vigilant; because your adversary the devil, as a roaring lion, walketh about, seeking whom he may devour.

1 John 3:8—He that committeth sin is of the devil; for the devil sinneth from the beginning. For this purpose the Son of God was manifested, that he might destroy the works of the devil.

1 John 5:18—We know that whosoever is born of God sinneth not; but he that is begotten of God keepeth himself, and that wicked one toucheth him not.

Revelation 12:10, 11—And I heard a loud voice saying in heaven, Now is come salvation, and strength, and the kingdom of our God, and the power of his Christ: for the accuser of our brethren is cast down, which accused them before our God day and night. And they overcame him by the blood of the Lamb, and by the word of their testimony; and they loved not their lives unto the death.

Selfishness

Proverbs 28:8—He that by usury and unjust gain increaseth his substance, he shall gather it for him that will pity the poor.

Acts 20:35—I have shewed you all things, how that so labouring ye ought to support the weak, and to re-

member the words of the Lord Jesus, how he said, It
is more blessed to give than to receive.

2 Corinthians 9:6, 7—But this I say, He which soweth
sparingly shall reap also sparingly; and he which
soweth bountifully shall reap also bountifully.
Every man according as he purposeth in his heart,
so let him give; not grudgingly, or of necessity: for
God loveth a cheerful giver.

1 Timothy 6:10—For the love of money is the root of all
evil: which while some coveted after, they have
erred from the faith, and pierced themselves
through with many sorrows.

Shame

Psalms 25:20—O keep my soul, and deliver me: let me
not be ashamed; for I put my trust in thee.

Psalms 31:1—In thee, O Lord, do I put my trust; let me
never be ashamed: deliver me in thy righteousness.

Romans 1:16—For I am not ashamed of the gospel of
Christ: for it is the power of God unto salvation to
every one that believeth; to the Jew first, and also to
the Greek.

Romans 5:5—And hope maketh not ashamed; because
the love of God is shed abroad in our hearts by the
Holy Ghost which is given unto us.

2 Timothy 2:15—Study to shew thyself approved unto
God, a workman that needeth not to be ashamed,
rightly dividing the word of truth.

1 Peter 4:16—Yet if any man suffer as a Christian, let
him not be ashamed; but let him glorify God on this
behalf.

1 John 2:28—And now, little children, abide in him; that, when he shall appear, we may have confidence, and not be ashamed before him at his coming.

Sickness

Psalms 103:3—Who forgiveth all thine iniquities; who healeth all thy diseases.

Psalms 147:3—He healeth the broken in heart, and bindeth up their wounds.

Proverbs 3:8—It shall be health to thy navel, and marrow to thy bones.

Proverbs 4:22—For they are life unto those that find them, and health to all their flesh.

Matthew 8:17—That it might be fulfilled which was spoken by Esaias the prophet, saying, Himself took our infirmities, are bare our sicknesses.

Mark 16:18—They shall take up serpents; and if they drink any deadly thing, it shall not hurt them; they shall lay hands on the sick, and they shall recover.

James 5:14—Is any sick among you? let him call for the elders of the church; and let them pray over him, anointing him with oil in the name of the Lord.

1 Peter 2:24—Who his own self bare our sins in his own body on the tree, that we, being dead to sins, should live unto righteousness: by whose stripes ye were healed.

Sin

Isaiah 43:25—I, even I, am he that blotteth out thy transgressions for mine own sake, and will not remember thy sins.

John 8:34—Jesus answered them, Verily, verily, I say unto you, Whosoever committeth sin is the servant of sin.

Romans 6:14—For sin shall not have dominion over you: for ye are not under the law, but under grace.

Romans 6:22—But now being made free from sin, and become servants to God, ye have your fruit unto holiness, and the end everlasting life.

James 4:17—Therefore to him that knoweth to do good, and doeth it not, to him it is sin.

James 5:20—Let him know, that he which converteth the sinner from the error of his way shall save a soul from death, and shall hide a multitude of sins.

1 John 2:1—My little children, these things write I unto you, that ye sin not. And if any man sin, we have an advocate with the Father, Jesus Christ the righteous.

1 John 5:17—All unrighteousness is sin: and there is a sin not unto death.

Slander

Exodus 20:16—Thou shalt not bear false witness against thy neighbour.

Psalms 31:20—Thou shalt hide them in the secret of thy presence from the pride of man: thou shalt keep them secretly in a pavilion from the strife of tongues.

Psalms 101:5—Whoso privily slandereth his neighbour, him will I cut off: him that hath an high look and a proud heart will not I suffer.

Proverbs 10:18—He that hideth hatred with lying lips, and he that uttereth a slander, is a fool.

Isaiah 54:17—No weapon that is formed against thee shall prosper; and every tongue that shall rise against thee in judgment thou shalt condemn. This is the heritage of the servants of the Lord, and their righteousness is of me, saith the Lord.

Sorrow

Psalms 34:18—The Lord is nigh unto them that are of a broken heart; and saveth such as be of a contrite spirit.

Psalms 42:11—Why art thou cast down, O my soul? and why art thou disquieted within me? hope thou in God: for I shall yet praise him, who is the health of my countenance, and my God.

Proverbs 10:22—The blessing of the Lord, it maketh rich, and he addeth no sorrow with it.

Proverbs 15:13—A merry heart maketh a cheerful countenance: but by sorrow of the heart the spirit is broken.

John 15:11—These things have I spoken unto you, that my joy might remain in you, and that your joy might be full.

Galatians 5:22—But the fruit of the Spirit is love, joy, peace, longsuffering, gentleness, goodness, faith.

Speech

Psalms 37:30—The mouth of the righteous speaketh wisdom, and his tongue talketh of judgment.

Psalms 141:3—Set a watch, O Lord, before my mouth; keep the door of my lips.

Proverbs 6:2—Thou art snared with the words of thy mouth, thou art taken with the words of thy mouth.

Proverbs 10:11—The mouth of a righteous man is a well of life: but violence covereth the mouth of the wicked.

Proverbs 12:6—The words of the wicked are to lie in wait for blood: but the mouth of the upright shall deliver them.

Proverbs 15:4—A wholesome tongue is a tree of life: but perverseness therein is a breach in the spirit.

Proverbs 16:23—The heart of the wise teacheth his mouth, and addeth learning to his lips.

Proverbs 18:21—Death and life are in the power of the tongue: and they that love it shall eat the fruit thereof.

Matthew 12:36—But I say unto you, That every idle word that men shall speak, they shall give account thereof in the day of judgment.

Matthew 15:11—Not that which goeth into the mouth defileth a man; but that which cometh out of the mouth, this defileth a man.

Mark 11:23—For verily I say unto you, That whosoever shall say unto this mountain, Be thou removed, and be thou cast into the sea; and shall not doubt in his heart, but shall believe that those things which he saith shall come to pass; he shall have whatsoever he saith.

Luke 6:45—A good man out of the good treasure of his heart bringeth forth that which is good; and an evil man out of the evil treasure of his heart bringeth forth that which is evil: for of the abundance of the heart his mouth speaketh.

1 Corinthians 10:10—Neither murmur ye, as some of them also murmured, and were destroyed of the destroyer.

Philippians 2:14—Do all things without murmurings and disputings.

Colossians 4:6—Let your speech be alway with grace, seasoned with salt, that ye may know how ye ought to answer every man.

2 Timothy 2:16—But shun profane and vain babblings: for they will increase unto more ungodliness.

1 Peter 3:10—For he that will love life, and see good days, let him refrain his tongue from evil, and his lips that they speak no guile.

Strife

Proverbs 16:28—A froward man soweth strife: and a whisperer separateth chief friends.

Proverbs 20:3—It is an honour for a man to cease from strife: but every fool will be meddling.

Philippians 2:3—Let nothing be done through strife or vainglory; but in lowliness of mind let each esteem other better than themselves.

2 Timothy 2:23—But foolish and unlearned questions avoid, knowing that they do gender strifes.

James 3:16—For where envying and strife is, there is confusion and every evil work.

T

Temptation

1 Corinthians 10:13—There hath no temptation taken you but such as is common to man: but God is faithful, who will not suffer you to be tempted above that ye are able; but will with the temptation also make a way to escape, that ye may be able to bear it.

James 1:2, 3—My brethren, count it all joy when ye fall into divers temptations; Knowing this, that the trying of your faith worketh patience.

James 1:13, 14—Let no man say when he is tempted, I am tempted of God: for God cannot be tempted with evil, neither tempteth he any man: But every man is tempted, when he is drawn away of his own lust, and enticed.

2 Peter 2:9—The Lord knoweth how to deliver the godly out of temptations, and to reserve the unjust unto the day of judgment to be punished.

Tithing

Proverbs 3:9, 10—Honour the Lord with thy substance, and with the firstfruits of all thine increase: So shall thy barns be filled with plenty, and thy presses shall burst out with new wine.

Malachi 3:8—Will a man rob God? Yet ye have robbed me. But ye say, Wherein have we robbed thee? In tithes and offerings.

Malachi 3:10—Bring ye all the tithes into the storehouse, that there may be meat in mine house, and prove me now herewith, saith the Lord of hosts, if I will not open you the windows of heaven, and pour you out a blessing, that there shall not be room enough to receive it.

Matthew 6:3, 4—But when thou doest alms, let not thy left hand know what thy right hand doeth: That thine alms may be in secret: and thy Father which seeth in secret himself shall reward thee openly.

Tribulation

Deuteronomy 4:30, 31—When thou art in tribulation, and all these things are come upon thee, even in the latter days, if thou turn to the Lord thy God, and shalt be obedient unto his voice; (For the Lord thy God is a merciful God;) he will not forsake thee, neither destroy thee, nor forget the covenant of thy fathers which he sware unto them.

John 16:33—These things I have spoken unto you, that in me ye might have peace. In the world ye shall have tribulation: but be of good cheer; I have overcome the world.

Romans 5:3—And not only so, but we glory in tribulations also: knowing that tribulation worketh patience.

Trouble

Psalms 9:9—The Lord also will be a refuge for the oppressed, a refuge in times of trouble.

Psalms 27:5—For in the time of trouble he shall hide me in his pavilion: in the secret of his tabernacle shall he hide me; he shall set me up upon a rock.

Psalms 34:17—The righteous cry, and the Lord heareth, and delivereth them out of all their troubles.

Psalms 41:1—Blessed is he that considereth the poor: the Lord will deliver him in time of trouble.

Proverbs 11:8—The righteous is delivered out of trouble, and the wicked cometh in his stead.

Proverbs 21:23—Whoso keepeth his mouth and his tongue keepeth his soul from troubles.

U

Uncleanness

Acts 10:28—And he said unto them, Ye know how that it is an unlawful thing for a man that is a Jew to keep company, or come unto one of another nation; but God hath shewed me that I should not call any man common or unclean.

Romans 14:14—I know, and am persuaded by the Lord Jesus, that there is nothing unclean of itself: but to him that esteemeth any thing to be unclean, to him it is unclean.

1 John 1:7—But if we walk in the light, as he is in the light, we have fellowship one with another, and the blood of Jesus Christ his Son cleanseth us from all sin.

1 John 3:2, 3—Beloved, now are we the sons of God, and it doth not yet appear what we shall be: but we know that, when he shall appear, we shall be like him; for we shall see him as he is. And every man that hath this hope in him purifieth himself, even as he is pure.

Understanding

Psalms 119:130—The entrance of thy words giveth light; it giveth understanding unto the simple.

Proverbs 2:11—Discretion shall preserve thee, understanding shall keep thee.

Proverbs 3:5—Trust in the Lord with all thine heart; and lean not unto thine own understanding.

Proverbs 3:13—Happy is the man that findeth wisdom, and the man that getteth understanding.

Proverbs 9:6—Forsake the foolish, and live; and go in the way of understanding.

Proverbs 19:8—He that getteth wisdom loveth his own soul: he that keepeth understanding shall find good.

Proverbs 28:5—Evil men understand not judgment: but they that seek the Lord understand all things.

2 Timothy 2:7—Consider what I say; and the Lord give thee understanding in all things.

V

Vengeance

Deuteronomy 32:35—To me belongeth vengeance and recompence; their foot shall slide in due time: for the day of their calamity is at hand, and the things that shall come upon them make haste.

Psalms 94:1, 2—O Lord God, to whom vengeance belongeth; O God, to whom vengeance belongeth, shew thyself. Lift up thyself, thou judge of the earth: render a reward to the proud.

Nahum 1:2—God is jealous, and the Lord revengeth; the Lord revengeth, and is furious; the Lord will take vengeance on his adversaries, and he reserveth wrath for his enemies.

Luke 18:7, 8—And shall not God avenge his own elect, which cry day and night unto him, though he bear long with them? I tell you that he will avenge them speedily. Nevertheless when the Son of man cometh, shall he find faith on the earth?

Romans 12:19—Dearly beloved, avenge not yourselves, but rather give place unto wrath: for it is written, Vengeance is mine; I will repay, saith the Lord.

Vigilance

Matthew 24:42—Watch therefore: for ye know not what hour your Lord doth come.

Luke 12:37—Blessed are those servants, whom the lord when he cometh shall find watching: verily I say unto you, that he shall gird himself, and make them to sit down to meat, and will come forth and serve them.

1 Thessalonians 5:6—Therefore let us not sleep, as do others; but let us watch and be sober.

Titus 2:13—Looking for that blessed hope, and the glorious appearing of the great God and our Saviour Jesus Christ.

2 Peter 3:10—But the day of the Lord will come as a thief in the night; in the which the heavens shall pass away with a great noise, and the elements shall melt with fervent heat, the earth also and the works that are therein shall be burned up.

Weakness

Psalms 27:1—The Lord is my light and my salvation; whom shall I fear? the Lord is the strength of my life; of whom shall I be afraid?

Psalms 29:11—The Lord will give strength unto his people; the Lord will bless his people with peace.

Psalms 46:1—God is our refuge and strength, a very present help in trouble.

Isaiah 40:31—But they that wait upon the Lord shall renew their strength; they shall mount up with wings as eagles; they shall run, and not be weary; and they shall walk, and not faint.

Matthew 11:28—Come unto me, all ye that labour and are heavy laden, and I will give you rest.

Colossians 1:11—Strengthened with all might, according to his glorious power, unto all patience and long-suffering with joyfulness.

Widow

Psalms 146:9—The Lord preserveth the strangers; he relieveth the fatherless and widow: but the way of the wicked he turneth upside down.

Proverbs 15:25—The Lord will destroy the house of the proud: but he will establish the border of the widow.

Isaiah 1:17—Learn to do well; seek judgment, relieve the oppressed, judge the fatherless, plead for the widow.

1 Timothy 5:3—Honour widows that are widows indeed.

James 1:27—Pure religion and undefiled before God and the Father is this, To visit the fatherless and widows in their affliction, and to keep himself unspotted from the world.

Wisdom

Psalms 51:6—Behold, thou desirest truth in the inward parts: and in the hidden part thou shalt make me to know wisdom.

Proverbs 3:7—Be not wise in thine own eyes: fear the Lord, and depart from evil.

Proverbs 3:15, 16—She is more precious than rubies: and all the things thou canst desire are not to be compared unto her. Length of days is in her right hand; and in her left hand riches and honour.

Proverbs 4:5—Get wisdom, get understanding: forget it not; neither decline from the words of my mouth.

Proverbs 24:5—A wise man is strong; yea, a man of knowledge increaseth strength.

1 Corinthians 1:30—But of him are ye in Christ Jesus, who of God is made unto us wisdom, and righteousness, and sanctification, and redemption.

Ephesians 1:17—That the God of our Lord Jesus Christ, the Father of glory, may give unto you the spirit of wisdom and revelation in the knowledge of him.

Colossians 2:3—In whom are hid all the treasures of wisdom and knowledge.

James 1:5—If any of you lack wisdom, let him ask of God, that giveth to all men liberally, and upbraideth not; and it shall be given him.

Worry

Psalms 55:22—Cast thy burden upon the Lord, and he shall sustain thee: he shall never suffer the righteous to be moved.

Galatians 6:2—Bear ye one another's burdens, and so fulfil the law of Christ.

Philippians 4:7—And the peace of God, which passeth all understanding, shall keep your hearts and minds through Christ Jesus.

1 Peter 5:7—Casting all your care upon him; for he careth for you.

Worship

Exodus 34:14—For thou shalt worship no other god: for the Lord, whose name is Jealous, is a jealous God.

Psalms 29:2—Give unto the Lord the glory due unto his name; worship the Lord in the beauty of holiness.

Psalms 95:6—O come, let us worship and bow down: let us kneel before the Lord our maker.

John 4:24—God is a Spirit: and they that worship him must worship him in spirit and in truth.

X

Xenophobia

Psalms 18:44, 45—As soon as they hear of me, they shall obey me: the strangers shall submit themselves unto me. The strangers shall fade away, and be afraid out of their close places.

Isaiah 25:5—Thou shalt bring down the noise of strangers, as the heat in a dry place; even the heat with the shadow of a cloud: the branch of the terrible ones shall be brought low.

Matthew 25:34, 35—Then shall the King say unto them on his right hand, Come, ye blessed of my Father, inherit the kingdom prepared for you from the foundation of the world: For I was an hungred, and ye gave me meat: I was thirsty, and ye gave me drink: I was a stranger, and ye took me in.

Hebrews 13:2—Be not forgetful to entertain strangers: for thereby some have entertained angels unawares.

3 John 5—Beloved, thou doest faithfully whatsoever thou doest to the brethren, and to strangers.

Y

Yoke

Isaiah 9:4—For thou hast broken the yoke of his burden, and the staff of his shoulder, the rod of his oppressor, as in the day of Midian.

Matthew 11:29, 30—Take my yoke upon you, and learn of me; for I am meek and lowly in heart: and ye shall find rest unto your souls. For my yoke is easy, and my burden is light.

Galatians 5:1—Stand fast therefore in the liberty where-with Christ hath made us free, and be not entangled again with the yoke of bondage.

Youth

Psalms 103:5—Who satisfieth thy mouth with good things; so that thy youth is renewed like the eagle's.

Ecclesiastes 11:9, 10—Rejoice, O young man, in thy youth; and let thy heart cheer thee in the days of thy youth, and walk in the ways of thine heart, and in the sight of thine eyes: but know thou, that for all these things God will bring thee into judgment. Therefore remove sorrow from thy heart, and put away evil from thy flesh: for childhood and youth are vanity.

Ecclesiastes 12:1—Remember now thy Creator in the days of thy youth, while the evil days come not, nor the years draw nigh, when thou shalt say, I have no pleasure in them.

1 Timothy 4:12—Let no man despise thy youth; but be thou an example of the believers, in word, in conversation, in charity, in spirit, in faith, in purity.

Z

Zeal

Titus 2:14—Who gave himself for us, that he might redeem us from all iniquity, and purify unto himself a peculiar people, zealous of good works.

Revelation 3:19—As many as I love, I rebuke and chasten: be zealous therefore, and repent.

You can own a complete BIBLE REFERENCE LIBRARY for under $15